END SONGS

Published in the United States by
Beckham Publications Group, Inc.
P.O. Box 4066, Silver Spring, MD 20914

ISBN: 0-9823876-3-6

Library of Congress Cataloging in Publication:

END SONGS

Followed by an essay, "The Crime of Prometheus"

Marjorie Burke Zittau

THE **Beckham**
PUBLICATIONS GROUP, INC.
Silver Spring

For

HERBERT ZITTAU

"THE SAME, THAT IS, TO REASON AND TO BE."
—Parmenides

The highest intelligence is love,
Which apprehends the divine in the other
And is thankful, as for a gift bestowed.

CONTENTS

END SONG

I lie upon your pyre

And a tendril of breath

Embraces the urn wherein repose

My ashen reveries.

FIRST LOVE

We gazed upon our gaze

In the pool of Narcissus

And awakened delicate blossoms;

Deep we drank of each other

And let our merged image

Dip into enchanted depths

Where no prying suns could reach.

THE BRIDEGROOM

I fear and desire your desire,

Dark, terrifying,

A storm

Tearing through tender flowers.

WE

We sat facing each other

And your words tasted of ambrosia,

Your voice transposed time into music.

The moment did not wait for us

Yet, once we feasted as gods

And that suffices.

THE POMEGRANATE TREE

Remember the pomegranate tree on the hill

That blew us crimson kisses in May

And spread its garlanded arms for shade,

Floating petals on our murmurs

That rippled through the ripening summer;

Soon autumn's cymbal clanged against

The brazen sky, setting wind and boughs

Awhir in fiery festival

While wine-ripe fruit bowed low to us

Now grateful to be harvested.

We shared the mortal offering

As we walked toward winter, but left behind

Some seeds unhusked for our return.

MINOTAUR

Our meeting was a paradox;

From poles opposed we approached our presence

And became each other's unseen guide,

Threading labyrinthine corridors

Which vein life's stately edifice

And foster ceremonial frolic

Wondrous to the wanderers

Oblivious to the feast that follows.

Meanwhile, the demi-beast abides,

Misbegotten, gnawing his surd,

Solitary, resentful, taunting,

Surly in his underworld,

Provoking his panicked pawns to probe

The limits of his endless maze

With charts compounding complexity

And proofs that project puzzles brightly

And knot infinite escapes to nowhere.

Our paths meshed, and as our eyes met

A shaft of being slashed the shadows

And we found our way into the open,

Rejoicing in the real revealed

And the blessed nearness of what is nearest.

Free. But how could we have failed to see

Those sisters waiting with their thread and shears?

ALCHEMY

Do not doubt, despite my frailty,

My constancy, accept this jewel

Forged in the alembic of love;

The fires fueled by my faults

Have fused that turgid conglomerate

Into this pure transparency.

HOME

You have gone, yet your love remains,

Crowning me in its halo

And cradling me in a hallowed home

With sustenance that never does degrade

So that lovers may always partake;

And you showed me the secret path

That leads to freedom from its bliss.

CYPRESSES

Beloved, wandering through Orkus' meadows

and the mourning poppies of oblivion,

fast you forget our radiant forest walks;

yet when we meet we shall reflesh remembrance,

twinned wayfarers retracing hasty time

until it halts at our ambled grove where we

bide the dateless dusk, with roots entwined.

TIME

Time, who marks the rate of ruin

Of every beguiling beginning given,

Plowing embers under rubble,

Snagged on your golden wing; amazed,

Headlong hasting Time backslid

To salvage your song in an urn of amber.

THE OTHER

Who is the one standing beside me now

Regarding my sorrow with a cold eye?

Yet, even in embalming sleep

Were you not always here, waiting,

Ever watching in unforgetfulness?

MAENAD

In the moon's shadow we

Who are not here tread the ground

Covering our layered love,

Which awaits its archaeology.

LOSS

You have gone

And my heart beats

Against an empty cage.

ABSENCE

Your absence is nearer than my thought

And more distant than infinity;

How can the void be so heavy

Where there is no moon?

PASSAGE

A boat bore you through the fiery gate

To where you have always been;

Even if my longing could evoke you

I would forbid your return,

Nor would I have you think on me—

For thinking does entail existence—

And I would not have you wander

Again in interminable answer.

EURIDICE

The god's gift dooms me

With your presence, your backward look,

Sun-strike on the stream

Thunder through the veins

Gold rain curtaining

Perspective and past

Plucked strings fusing

Frayed quarters into cosmos

Kindling the stars

To illumine

From the center they shroud

Their slow burn

Where I linger.

NIOBE

Look, pebbled paths point

Past rows of sculpted yew

To my heart's tomb there

Below the pulsing fountain

That drains melodious streams

Into infinity's dribble.

THE GARDEN

My garden blooms bright in the springtime sun

So why do its flowers seem to be wearing mourning

And plaiting funeral wreaths for a sun eclipsed?

QUESTIONS

By some chance lapse of focus

Within your new dimension do you

In habit's thrall reflect on me?

Or does some root-tag tug you down

Toward earth's abyssmal ecstasy?

The wake of your implacable passage

Sucked the breath out of the sky.

Yet, if you feel the faintest fault

In the frozen void that parts us now

Let the shade of your thought slip through

And a world will fill the interval.

EVOCATION

In Hades, do not mourn for me

For I have grown fat on phantoms

Since you sailed into forgetfulness;

But you have been remembered, with ruddy libations,

And now you can yearn, and there is the danger.

STARS

Slinking like thieves among the shadows

Seeking the fire sighted from afar

On the starred brow of each other

We took the long chance; on the horizon

The bare peak rose and the vulture watched

While we hid the purloined spark

In the hollow reed of solitude;

We bear its stigma and endure

Unto the end we are marked for.

THE POET

While Pan sleeps the Dryad's lover stirs

And his embrace will loose her wooden bonds

For fledgling words to flutter their leafy perch

Then wing their song up to an aerial crown;

But the poet wants the nymph's profundity;

His kiss sounds her taproot and imprints his rune;

Deep is her delight, deeper than the day,

Awake in his dream, she wraps herself in shade.

THE FAUN OF PRAXITILES

Your smile has touched the delicate lip of the flute,

Drawing its tone, seductive, through the thickets

And corroded bastions of the mind

To open the view of a vineyard as yet without vintage

But ripening now for revelers, their limbs

Entwined with tendrils and becoming the vine

Heavy with clusters ready for the stomp of feet

So that wine can flow again and thoughts can dance.

PHIDIAS

It is a fine art of concealment

That casts nudity like a robe

Around the human body to adorn

So that it seems the essence of nature

In that it awakens awareness of essence;

The artist is molding the human form

Freed from its shadow of generation

Enlightening that intelligence

Which has carved its face and history,

As if a god transports the body

Into his radiant presence and composes

The strife of instincts so that all the limbs

Repose as though desires had fully feasted

In harmony to hallow reason's image.

THE WARRIORS OF RIACE

Who can find the bright and holy words

To evoke Hellas again?

And if a god appeared who

Could suffer its presence, uncanny,

It's shock, the trembling, the terror,

Without the intercession of the artist

Making its power manifest as beauty?

Warriors, envoys of art's golden age

Hewn out of leaden time,

You held passage to the sacred cities

Of Italy's shores, but their reefs

Delayed your destiny,

And you waited out millennia,

With the wreckage, under the deep waters

And below the waves of war that razed

Those colonies of ancient fame.

Now you are rescued from oblivion

In your primal, undaunted glory,

And lift a corner of the veil of barbarism

Under which we cower.

THE OLIVE TREE

Who can fathom the light

Of the olive tree,

Its speckled space embranching

A vanished age of silver

That we can enter only here.

NEREID

As a wave that pounds against a rock,

Repelled, recruits its force from rising tide,

Here am I, cast at your feet again,

So bend your loftiness, my love, one time

To lift me to your heart before the ebb

Pulls me back into the boundless night.

DIOSCURI

To solace and righten the storm-tossed

Your hands touch over so many waves

Which cruelly press each forward swell

Down into the sea's oblivion

Then urge each following wave forward;

They plash this way and that, whipped up

By every passing gale and swerved

By any wandering influence;

But the constant circles of your souls

Eddy far above, from fixed centers,

And verge gently, even as they turn,

Their rays advancing toward themselves alone.

(for Michael and John Mepham)
(First published in the Classical Outlook)

APHAIA OF AEGINA

Scene: The deserted remains of the fifth-century B.C. temple in the island of Aegina. Behind it, the sun is setting in the Aegean Sea. The chorus of the votaries of Hecate is disposed among the Columns.

Chorus:

Fleeing Cretan Minos,

Aphaia dived into the speckled wave

And rode the dragon's flank,

But Nereus' daughters caught her falling

And gave their green cave's sanctuary.

Aiacus' pebbled shore she chose

And seized on our surmounting grove,

Ground deeded to us of old,

Blasting hallowed rights of blood and kinship.

Who knows whence she came,

By what authority,

Of what lineage?

And now her temple is rubble

And she cannot be seen.

But here comes her last priest,

Half-crazed with searching for her,

Who will have no part of our sacred rites.

Priest:

(walks to the altar at the end of the temple)

Who is lonlier than a god alone?

You must do your own chores,

Talk to yourself

And water your own grove.

Oh bride of desolation,

Who will worship you when I am gone?

Chorus:

See, how haggard is this pious priest.

His god-gluttony beggars him.

To worship her is to belong nowhere.

He wanders in deepening shadows

Of her receding light.

Priest:

My worship is to restore to the god of her own.

See, I press honey on her altar stone

And wreathe it with crocuses covering her floor.

(lifting his hands)

Rose of fire, self-grown,

What can I do but tend

To tasks you never require?

I bring water in an urn

Not for your thirst

But for my own.

Daily I shoulder this hollow vessel

And fill it at your fountain.

What abyss engenders my dire thirst?

At dawn when I purify your precinct

And over my hands your fountain vents

Its joyous self-illustrations

Could I but pin my happiness, then,

Like a rose, in your hair.

Aphaia, you only gift I crave,

See how I spill my coffers on your floor,

Annoint you, pour out all my pearls,

And empty-handed beg to give you more,

For all my gifts were thievings from your grove.

Shall I forbid the sky to press upon you?

The fountain at your feet drips drowsiness.

Cool is the underside of leaves

And your columns are rooted

In honeycombs of heavenly bees.

Chorus:

Will you yet not regard our wrongs,

Heavy with the increase of time?

Priest:

What is yours is not taken from you.

Chorus:

Foul litter insults our altars.

No libations, no reverence are given us.

Our anguish is the ferment of our wine;

Our curses carouse in festive unforgetting.

The usurper of our apportioned power,

Though she be hidden, we still pursue.

Priest:

She will reappear always,

And you will be kept at bay.

(muses at the altar)

I was pre-empted for your priesthood

From the beginning, Aphsia.

Under the serene gaze of your fountain's eye

I polished the mirrors of my mind.

Even while this band of ancient night-dwellers

Reached out for me from their phlegmatic dream

I lived inviolate.

Yet I am filled with dread.

Why was I chosed for this service?

I am your robe of darkness;

All my candles are ablaze

But chaos is in my heart.

I am the temple bereft of its god,

I am the desire that will survive.

What back-breaking toil I undergo

To earn my daily ambrosia.

Give back my mortality, Aphaia.

Let me die.

Heart of my madness,

All-conquering me,

Cold to my embrace

A perfect column

Not to be compassed.

Your violent grace destroys me.

Yet at your rocky feet gush

Springs of healing water.

I am heavy with you, Aphaia,

I know not where to shift my precious pain.

Each dawn you are reborn through me

And sink in me your fathomless weight each night.

Yet whence come you,

Born as fire through me?

Chorus:

Are you a vessel of gold?

Not once in lovely grottoes were

You one of us, our unslaked woe

In asking now for vengeance' cup

Crowned with blood, so can you pluck

Out of your own breast's breathless damp

Your burning sun to still our thirst?

The day can never penetrate

Our profundity nor our

Never oblivious sleep

Which nourishes desire's fundament

Feeding the topmost fruit

Of the tree you feed upon.

Love of the god will send you back to us

For its digs its own pit

And its extremity of servitude

begets self-loathing.

The hook in the heart

That will pull you

Against your will

Even unto our depths.

Priest:

Never.

I can forgo the use of my desire

Yet I shall abide here.

Shining one, let my midwife mind

Hold up to you a mirror

Wherein you may preen yourself.

Though I cannot look at you

But from the distance of my dreaming

I can lay yellow roses at your feet

And then clear your path.

Yet whence come you?

A god exiled from peers—

Look upon me, another fugitive,

An isle anchored in the sea

To conjure you, receive you, bring you forth.

Chorus:

She eludes us but is not gone;

She will return not to abide;

Her temple of noble conception

And her garden feel our poison swell

Its veins with torpor that will not kill

While dew wrung from our frenzied limbs

Feeds fret of flowers frail as sighs.

But look, the matriarchal night

Is beckoning home her stars,

And you are pale and you have drawn

A hood around your head and shun

The white stare of the moon that spies

With malign chlorotic eye

Into your unroofed sanctum tracking

Rout upon the temple stairs

Where many-footed madness riots.

Priest:

Night, and I lie in the dust

The god has left.

Yet do not tempt me,

My desire, with hope,

Feed me no phantasms,

For I will snatch the bait

More savagely than Tantalus.

So, send no golden apples' scent

I, too, once dined at a god's table

And would shame now to own that

I raven for your spectral scraps.

Chorus:

Desires, and most of all, pure desires,

Are the threads with which we weave nets,

And you shall not slip away from us.

Priest:

You can never possess what never was yours.

Chorus:

You have power that makes you helpless before us.

In your ecstasy and in her possession of you

We shall catch also her and drive her forth

And then we can take back our own.

Like the ghost of a sun

She will moor ashen sails on the western shore.

Priest:

(lifts his face to the dark sky)

She will return, as music over the waters.

You shall never touch her,

For I declare her free of my bondage.

Nor shall what is hers become yours.

Now my words breathe lighter,

Borne by a north wind from its clear source,

Which errs neither in itself nor in its issue.

Ah, goddess, the fetters of the will are breaking.

I am becoming the sacrifice and the deity.

I am the libation accepted by Hades' dead.

I am Eros, too, and I am the desired.

I am the victim and I am also the victor.

I am the world and I am the awakened.

And you will rise again to enlighten

And to bear the Self's own child.

DELOS

There were feasts,

Dancing, fires, Apollo,

They blended lyres.

Long Ionian folds

White as foam

Trailed over bronze

glint of light on the shore,

turned, swept,

moved to your door.

Men, youths, wives,

Children awed,

Wended to throne,

site of the god,

paused

at the temple stair;

reverence

was graven there.

They brought offerings,

Wine

In great urns

smoke of chine;

they bore gold flowers alone

they laid gold nectar on stone.

I passed through the columns

And the throng of men,

Past the fires, feasts, flowers,

To find your sanctuary

And lay on your altar my song.

ARIADNE

From the desire of nectar

I became addicted to poison

That gripped me in a tightening web of nerves;

Yet by what lore, my love,

Did you gain the secret of my heart

And never did become lost in the maze of my passion

If not by the thread I handed you?

ARIADNE AT NAXOS

Radiant and ripe with the god you sat across from me then

And with delicate fingers decked the altar of day;

On your bright lips a smile spread over the meaning

of forgotten holy things not yet dreamed;

Of these you spoke, resonant with power from

the luminous one

who lives in the grape and its still, dark root;

The cymbal of your heart had struck noon and homes

and fields were abandoned,

The ground was reddened with wine and joyous riot;

The white bull bellowing in the hills was wreathed

as bridegroom

And the ardor in his veins beat distant drums;

Where then were the chains deeds dreamed they had fastened?

As we danced to this music from the world's first round

Night and dreamless sleep bound us in ivy clusters

of profound encounters and fathomless ravishment.

CITHAERON

Dawn kindles my mountain altar

and clouds of roses rise;

down the shrouded slopes descends

the vine god, treading sleep-bound roots

in the valley still buried in night,

and yet deeper below,

into more distant intimacy,

into the chalice of the inmost heart

he sinks, into the luminous,

all unseen, wreathing it with nectar,

so that the ancient stock swells with joy

and puts forth radiant clusters

to ripen, and thankful leaves.

ENDYMION

Long we lay on the forest floor

Eavesdropping on our angels' love;

Shadows of their winged words

Drifted whispering down the river.

Side by side, fearing to stir,

We dreamed separate dreams of waking

To see our angels in large, pure light.

Leaves fell from the autumn sun

And buried us beneath their quiet;

When the green river ceased to flow

We bade each other sleep no more:

Then, one long waking look we won

Of us alone, on blue peaks above,

Parting in luminous desolation.

DANAID

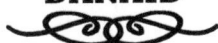

In Hades I have no rest for I must daily dip

An empty urn into the fountain which always flows

And my bridegroom waiting nearby fills me my cup and shows

The wound I gave him opening like a morning rose;

Then the hydra hiding in my thirst begins to rip

And slash my brimming vessel and fifty mouths affix

Which suck the eternal waters down into the Styx

Before one precious drop can ever reach my lip.

ORPHEUS

My love, what charm did Hades' music hold
To pull you back into his shadowy hall.
Was our ascent too steep, the sun too bold,
my song less joyous or less magical?
Along the darkly glistening Acheron
a pleasure boat is drifting without anchor
past scenes of glamorous transformation
where memory dissolves itself in languor.
Do you glide with spellbound motion in that keel,
your hand skimming the water, leaving no trace,
seduced by pleasures you can never feel,
taking fruits without eating, gifts without grace?
Oh, loss absolute, never again
may I open the door of day for you below,

nor may you life your face to mine when

my music woos you in the underglow.

For even while you sank in earth's dark veins

Clouds of madness gathered around my head,

now Maenads loose me from my living chains

and I hear my lyre playing to the dead.

SPARTA

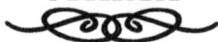

Grey-green olive trees, row upon row of them,

Cleave the red earth with implacable roots

and weave a crown for Spartan heroes

guarding in Elysium;

seed of their sacramental life is stored here,

the portion they reserved for gods withdrawn

in bliss to their intimate abode of Being

and no longer visible or heard from now;

for their season of return, heroes are needed,

and in their absence, too, serenely abiding

in justice's antique music and command

to shield a seer's envisaged fatherland.

ATHENA

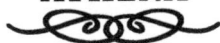

Who, if you appeared again, would give you ground,

daughter of the day god, and then who could abide

your presence;

who would become unveiled for that luminous encounter

to become a conversation with your logos, the sounding

of reason,

in an unconcealment of its own identity;

who would not retreat toward the refuge of opening space

and time's involutions into the familiar world at hand;

and yet where should we be at home if not on your ground

and what more familiar than our own Self planted there?

Once, you initiated the men you made your own

into a festival, a divine game of language,

where the players name essences of what is,

thus drawing them back to the point of Being

on which they depend.

Then projecting them into duality's mirror to create a world

of images discriminating its images;

for you wakened in them reason, the eye that unshrouds

the day

with the very atmosphere of its obscurity,

specious points gravely erring into matter,

by superimposing forms of being upon Being

in the ritual of your religion, science of what is real;

and so that the gods' speech could be heard also here,

proclaiming that to reason and to be are the same;

and so that its memory may hover in ever-present reflection,

upon its resonance a temple was reared for you.

Unnurtured, alone unborn from the confounding of what

is with what is not,

you descended like a star, rifting the clouds of worlds;

a star, not because you had dross to burn away

like spirits being purified to die or like lovers

loving to be transcended and mistaking the purgatorial

fires they kindle in each other's spellbound eyes;

you neither offered nor measured love's retribution;

the arrows of your desire over-reached love's farthest mark

to find the hearth of Self-sustaining fire to temper them

against Poseidon's bolts that blazed his turbulent will.

Your awesome adversary hurled his trident then

to rouse his horse, and the sea floor shook beneath hoof-beats

thundering the god's exaltation in his creature

as he fathomed his own mightiness in the stallion;

eyeless deep-sea hunters awoke at the bottom of night

and all the rivers of existence that had overflowed

their richness into glittering, stagnant pools where sharks hide

were churned into the torrent and cleansed of their debris

so that the horse, oppressed by superabundant nature

and the three-pronged goad that burrowed in its flank,

flailed its limbs against its own lashings and the foam

and whipped itself loose from the swaddling

bands of the ocean

to break trembling into the barren generality of sky,

where refugee spirit is free to prey upon itself;

then its back arched a firmament, its head a dawn,

and the bright air polished its senses so that its eyes

became suns

to search the ascetic pastures, and with its new-born breath it tested the undulant azure of an alien home.

Such was the creature in its splendid anarchy,

difficult to saddle and, at its ripest,

but ready for sacrifice, the offering of Poseidon.

Next, you brought forth your offerings, fruit

of austere thought,

that won the victory yet robbed the god of nothing

while it crowned his sacrifice and brought

the indomitable stallion

bridled willingly back into its home in Being

and made its master even of its own over-reaching.

In subterranean temples chthonic powers uprose,

Dreading the ruin of ancient shrines, ancestral tombs,

and metallic ages whence the great smith forged webs of weal,

bonds secure, and the wine-god's rites that unraveled them.

None of these you dislodged, but confirmed

each in its due place,

Giving Prometheus a precinct in the shadow of your science,

Civilizing Furies with praise of what their office meant,

and fixing the immemorial festivals of the year with its seasons

that console amidst the vagaries of nature and pledge of death.

Thus you righted old familiar deities in their rightness

and let all the powers come forth in your procession,

unshackled of error and invested monstrosity, transformed

without magic perpetually into what they really were,

being garlanded with the justice that secures your citadel.

And even now from your reserve your gifts appear

so that, though you are silent, we can still speak of you;

but who has fathomed fully the mystery of your olive tree

lifting its torches into the day, disclosing

to us our own luminosity?

(for Michael Anthony Kerrigan)

WOOING OF THE SPHINX

Once, on barren rocky perch

Athwart, your pit, you serenaded

Thebes' sacred seven-gated body.

Sired by your dragon-mother's son,

Old mother-vengeance you cried on us:

"Should son of Cadmus' plow dare father

Son of mine, he dies by his hand.

Mine alone is the fruit of my furrow,

To mend my wound and salve my sorrow."

You are nesting now in velvet hills

To hatch the fratricidal brood

Of dragon teeth that Cadmus sowed

Once in Thebes' incestuous earth.

Inviolable maid, ultimate nurse,

Self-perpetuating and primeval parent,

You abode with us before the beginning,

Warding the sinister gate of rebirth.

Your smile is poised for a kiss of the void;

Thirsty, we suck your lips sweet poison,

Drain your subtle song's dispason

Of lullabies, of lasting play time,

Of rivers that rolic with laughless mirth

And groves where each narcotic grows.

Self-comfortor, more than mother,

We drink from your eyes brimming with space

And then sink spellbound on your breast,

Our gaze rapt on the riddle you crowch over,

The seen unseen, unveiled in the dream.

You bind us to gods horizons gird

While we chase phantasms through your haunches,

Gorge on giant horns of plenty

In a manic myopia of childhood.

You clove Thebes' sheltering shield of kings;

With father's swords we rive our bread

And father's bread galls us to eat.

The infant in the ancient longs

To quicken the tomb, and to you turns.

So let your shadowy winds seduce us

With unawakening caresses;

Cradle us in your lethal lap

And hold us in unrebellious cords;

Reclaim us to your ancient stock

Whereon we leaf now, sterile grafts,

Sprung, they say, from a god's on-breathing

Borne by a flight of wayward breezes;

But your bowels, rooted in dragon earth,

Bind your wing's abysmal rounds,

And death's hound whimpers in your throat.

Oedipus looked upon your secret

With kingly eyes and spoke it out.

Nake, mutilated, yet maiden,

You wrapped your shame in oblivion.

He slew you with his second sight,

Blind to the act that gave him eyes;

Your riddle had come to roost in his crime.

A man of light, he walked in darkness,

And he knew not how he knew you,

Nor how he avenged you, dread songbird,

Unfathering fatherland, the orphan

Orphaning, with shears that shore you.

Royal ritual condemned him

To sacrilege profound, and a god

Nurtured in him a crimson vine.

We break its branches for a fire

To purify a foreign hearth;

You rise again among the hills

To fetch us home with velvet paws.

AUTUMN OAK

The cool whisper in the afternoon

Foretells the icy trumpeter and end

Of budding and busy forgetfulness so soon

And winds beneath which weary branches bend;

Still, my trunk may sheathe a now unborn

Ungenerated memory unknown

And it may waken in my sleep its form

And from my hibernation step full-grown.

HOMER

Like the sun, ever anew you make

A world of beauty where the gods can play

And Plato the demi-god can contemplate.

EPICURUS

Serenely nested in his void

The dark bird of freedom finely

Pecked apart all my treasures

Except the jewel of loneliness.

HEALER

Your eyes were clear lakes

Where the wondrous and innocent life

That dwelt within your indwelling vision

Was nourished and befriended by your art

Until the always undershadowing blight

And pain's incomprehensible indictment

Sank it under a tide of tears.

(for Elizabeth McKenna, M.D.)

THE APPLE TREE

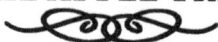

The apple tree blossomed yesterday

And now its fruit, unpicked,

Has fallen on the ground.

Hades also never hurries

To gather up his glorious harvest

Which lies, scattered, low

Upon oblivion's latitude.

(for William McKenna, M.D.)

COUNTERPARTS

You curl up on your cushion and your polished eyes
Reflect glacial pools where ancestral snow-tigers
In their high solitude are stalking antelope;
Your glance discovers me, too, with ancient kindred,
Hunting on hills of Helicon the Muses' game.

(for Melissa)

THE NAMING

The stag sprang from the red noon-tide

Bringing the hunter the shaft that he needs,

Angelic, the gift of naming, keen

To scent prey, ward by word

And fence the field of gathering names;

The hunters, spreading nets to herd them,

Spun from the shadowless point of noon,

Caught that big game which outlives living,

The theorem, master and dispenser of names;

The hunter then offered a feast of thanksgiving

That language had made life sacramental.

Yet, what furnace forged the garb

That bade death taste its mortal bite,

The noumenal ray which etched the rune-stone,

Carved the blazoned triumphal column,

Plucked a paean from vagrant air

And ripped illusion's laminates

To reveal close meaning, one's real owning?

THE CRIME OF PROMETHEUS

Tragedy, the art of Dionysus, has been variously defined in aesthetic terms, and poets as well as critics do lament its conspicuous absence, in aesthetic terms, as if this lost art form only waited for a poet to recall it to the aesthetic fold. At the present time, when the historical panorama of art is spread out as the Impressive if somewhat motley backdrop of an enlightened age, a facile and ingenious taste may derive some pleasurable excitement from the contemplation of an obsolete art and even believe that the melancholy sweetness evoked is attributable to the art itself and not to the fact that the art is so irretrievably distant, as is the tragic drama.

Greek tragedy was a short-lived phenomenon. It has been widely imitated, both in ancient and in modern times, and has stimulated new forms of dramatic expression. Tragedy itself, exquisite and late born, Athens' violet crown, perished in its very fulfillment, to the perpetual regret of subsequent aestheticians, whose historically trained glance has never discovered another art that could provide so much "disinterested" pleasure as the Greek drama and who, from their serene distance from the Greek scene, have spared no pains in attempting to account for the origin and characteristics of this unique art.

The mask of Greek tragedy, however, now belongs to a ghost, rising on the horizon of the past with ghosts of misty ancient gods, and it is no longer worn by actors of the living scene. Hence, the form of tragedy appears, from the vast distance, a mere illusion, a free form available to any audience disposed by a minimum of antiquarian lore to feel an Epicurean thrill of sadness in the contemplation of lost beauty, to which it seems to be transported, privately, by but a small cooperation of fancy.

Yet, after all, what must be the purpose of an art which is cultivated, just for its own sake, by an audience predisposed to sympathy and yet expecting from the art no substantial gain? Whence the quality of "disinterest" that is the virtue of the modern audience—an audience whose fervor in defending artistic license is fully equaled by its aversion to any consideration of the moral aim of art? Indeed, the audience has good cause, if not substantial logical support, for its disinterested purity. Though its conscience does not restrain it from a playful intimacy with the imaged forms of art reminiscent of the craft of idolatry, which once fundamentally characterized the practice of those "fine" arts, its virtue, requiring the suppression of idolatry, can be credited with the modern ambivalence regarding the value of art as well as for doctrines that treat the aesthetic as a special philosophical category.

In short, an explanation of art that will set it apart from technical and scientific knowledge, as well as from ethical practice, has been found necessary to absolve the modern audience of responsibility for works of magic, witchcraft, and image-worship, along with the other paraphernalia useful in interceding with a spirit, all of which constituted the primitive tools of art. The resultant notions of free or disinterested pleasure that pervade aesthetic doctrine seem to guarantee that the modern audience can taste of forbidden experience in all innocence.

The Greeks acknowledged many gods, and their art, the only honest European art, was candidly a devotional offering and supplication to the gods as well as an intricate magical snare to keep these divine beings benign and communicative with the earth. For this purpose of spiritual persuasion or coercion, the imaged human body, the supreme sacramental vessel, was most instrumental. To become a god—this was the aim of the Greek way of life. If one has been robbed of this aim, however, and has been forbidden the use of images in religious practice,

Greek art must constitute a spiritual crime. Yet, could this art be cultivated purely for its own sake or for curiosity's sake, as a mere commodity of knowledge, it would then entail no guilt and would be spiritually uncompromising. To serve art, though, and not its gods—has one ever done so without peril either to his conscience or to his art? At any rate, as a result of an historical-Epicurean point of view that regards art variously as illusion, the free product of fancy, a picture of life, or as tonic to the emotions, the stature of the ancient tragedies has diminished, even though amidst the tenderest regard, in proportion to the distance and the disinteredness through which they are surveyed.

The ghost of tragedy may haunt our theatres occasionally, but its altar is tended elsewhere. Texts may be studied and glossed, but a Greek tragedy cannot be contained by a text and much less can it be translated onto a page. Greek tragedy was, above all, a festival of seeing, a carnival, a plot for making a god visible, and it was celebrated in broad daylight under the open sky. Modern taste, which prefers to take its aesthetic fare in privacy and darkness for the sake of a heightened illusion of naturalism and for a freer play of fantasy, is too dainty to relish the sanguinary products of tragic artifice.

Drama, ancient or modern, is nevertheless a spectacle of the human scene, designed for the public at large. The Athenian public, at home in the market place or assembly, was a notoriously word-intoxicated audience and one that never ceased to admire the Word. Of all marvels, human speech, the witness of reason, seemed to them the most wonderful, because it was the instrument which could mediate between men and gods. And because they believed, therefore, that conversation was a way over which truth could be tracked down, the Athenians resorted to the public places in order to speak and to listen to speech.

The modern public, composed of great urban masses that drift like sand among rocks, is strangely silent in contrast. It seems preoccupied, abstracted, and plunged into reverie. Along innumerable orderly streets these masses hurry on unapparent and mysterious quests, moving from place to place, roving over an increasingly flattened landscape. Although their goal is unknown, the roads thereto are marvelously smooth. A faith in the ultimate beneficent external ordering of ways and means of living has replaced the ancient faith in thought and discourse as the free man's instruments for obtaining the life of reason. The modern masses are bound to be happy. They are chained by adamantine laws through which a lone and concealed and increasingly abstract spiritual force becomes manifest.

This alteration in spiritual direction has a source and symbol in Prometheus on the rock, punished for a crime of such magnitude that he inspired never-ending terror in the Greeks, yet he elicits only pity from the modern man.

Of all the heroes brought forth upon the Attic stage, the giant Prometheus represented man in his largest dimension: and in his vastest capacity for suffering. Certainly the dark enigmatical Titan of Aeschylus' tragedy was the most spectacular as well as the most monstrous of the tragic offerings.

The daimon Prometheus was the son of earth and a brother of those Titans who had castrated their father and had fallen thus under their father's curse to the effect that none of them should succeed him. In the Titans' war against the Olympian gods Prometheus had betrayed his brothers and had aligned himself with the gods. Though he had used all his guile in the defeat of his fellow Titans the gods had, even so, rejected the victor's claim of this ungodly magician-priest, and he had remained portionless in their estate. Crafty counselor to the gods, he was barred from enjoying their rights. From his brothers, whom he had brought low, he was eternally estranged. He was Prometheus the fateless.

Prometheus, arrogant, revengeful, all-knowing, and wrathful, was a dangerous exile from divine communion, a daimon hovering between heaven and earth, brooding over his anguished pride and loneliness. From the depths of his misery Prometheus looked down upon the race of earth-men, remnants of the Titan spawn, whom Zeus' victory had doomed to extinction along with the entire Titanic generation.

Left reliant solely on their natural capacities, these men-had rapidly sunk into a savage mode of life. Depraved, hopeless, under the shadow of death, they were men without necessity, men without a story. It was precisely because they were fatherless and in need that Prometheus saw in them his instrument of revenge.

Henceforth Prometheus made them his ally. Possessing nothing of his own, forced into exile, he determined to create his own lawless kingdom out of the thievings from his enemies. He resolved secretively to subvert the new Olympian realm and to save the race of earth-men.

So he stole the fire of Zeus. He stole his creative power. He shook the Olympian throne. For it had been Zeus' design to beget a new race of higher men, sacramental men, men born of his fire. Prometheus robbed these divine men of their paternity. He carried off Zeus' fire in a hollow navel-reed in order that he himself could be reborn as a son of Olympus. He contrived for himself a second birth, an unprecedented crime.

Prometheus' great hubris consisted in his far-reaching subversion of divine order. Not only did he possess creative fire, but he also gave it to men. He thereby prolonged the time-cycle of the Titanic race and prevented the emergence of the higher man. His punishment was that he must be chained to that cycle.

Hence, to the Greeks, Prometheus was a most awful figure of guilt, suffering a punishment which, though just, was terrifying to contemplate. This first rebel slave was author of our foredoomed race. He had taken by adaption the tribe of fateless, superfluous earth-men who had rushed headlong into nothingness, unsubstantial as shadows, and he had placed this rubble into the fire of his spiritual theft, like pots, to give them fine finish and the illusory appearance of the obverted sacramental man. Thus were they born again, these creatures of Prometheus, as works of art.

Then Prometheus offered up his resurfaced Titan-men as a burnt offering of appeasement to Zeus, lord of gods. But Zeus spurned his gift. He saw that these men had been merely wrapped in a veil of magic, not reborn in substance. They had not blood good enough for his taste. Prometheus had not only stolen fire but had perverted its use to artistic deception.

Thus was Prometheus chained to the rock for making spurious sacrifice. Therefore this artisan of men had no temples built him and no worship accorded him on earth, although his creatures survived and multiplied. For, Prometheus could give them no paternity. The Titan father had been overthrown and with him their inheritance. Prometheus the portionless was a mere artist, a maker of illusions, who worked with pilfered scraps of earth and fire. He spread anarchy. He asserted not only men's freedom from paternal law but also their right to steal another's heritage. For, further to subvert Zeus' power, Prometheus, son of Titan Earth, worked to restore the ancient mother-right and the brotherhood of her sons. He instituted "natural" right as a legal claim against divine right.

Was not Earth, Maia, mistress of magic and mother of all, now their only parent? Could not the brothers found a universal motherhood in which each could have his part? Prometheus would teach them the old earth-wisdom, Maya-magic, as the means thereto.

So he made them wise in her wisdom, bestowing on them the machinery of nature-knowledge. He taught them how to find their way through the world. He taught them how to assemble parts of stone, wood, and metal for the control of their environment. He taught them how to put words together and then to translate these words into things in order to penetrate nature's secrets. He taught them religious techniques by which they might raise themselves to a speaking level with gods. Before Prometheus, men had possessed no story, no past, no myth. Nothing had ever happened to them Prometheus' culture-crime is the root of the most ancient European mythos.

Prometheus, in transforming the world into a magical scene for his men, also pointed the way for its continuance through a technological brotherhood of men, a lure that always lies ready at hand for the disinherited in that it promises each a part of nature's possession. He thereby began to bind them, with himself, faster to the Maya-matrix, who ever strives to gain power through her sons in their overthrow of paternal rule. Seducing by new scenes and continuously novel transfigurations, she clasps them securely while she invites them to possess that which is nothing to own. For she is but illusion. She can never yield men a portion of herself. She can never be known. She can never give them mastery. She can bequeath no inheritance. She is able but to put men in ceaseless motion in quest of her, over ways which lead nowhere except to her further phantasmagoria. She spurs them on to discover, through motion, the center of matter in its formal duality. A vain search. For, had matter a center it would be at rest. Though they father new sons for her maintenance of mother-right through the brotherhood of man, through her is brought to pass the ancient Titan curse that when the father's order is overturned the sons must divide their inheritance by the sword. She is now their only shared lot. Men without father and fatherland, though, constitute a brotherhood of betrayal. They are prepared to destroy one another at the first opportunity offered of grasping power over the earth.

Accordingly, each son is portionless except for his right over the mother, yet he learns that a part of her is nothing to possess unless he obtains the whole, and so he tries to own her by devising a formula that will yield him the totality of her parts—the illusion of illusions! In line with this he obliges himself to act in the name of the totality of his brothers in establishing a universal technological tyranny. Hence is inflamed is him that prurient egotism that desires to embrace the entire universe of time and space as its portion and but wastes energy and erodes the will for no real gain. In his predatory quest through the transformations of matter for the real matrix of rest and order each[1] brother walks alone, yet with the despotically felt duty to progress forward in the name of all his fellow men, rivals with universal claims equal in right to his. The brothers, thus turned over to nature, are made by nature separate, solitary, hostile, each compelled to give battle to the other for his inheritance, and are also made, by nature, brothers in bondage, each direly needing the amalgamation of all the others into a mass-society of incessant mobility and variance. For, according to ancient mother-right, no single brother will ever become master. The same technology which is the condition of universal brotherhood, with its irresponsible and exclusive right of force, insidiously disarms each.

The more Prometheus strove to forward his technological monolith in his conspiracy against Zeus, the tighter he bound himself to the shadows of earth and the more unspeakable became his torment of solitude among the earth-men. He was a god and longed to dwell among peers. He had held fire; now he lay in darkness. He raged with contradictory desires: to be free; to be a god on high; to bring Zeus down low with him. He wished to be saved from the nightmare of his own artful creation.

Once his mother had whispered to him in secret that even Zeus, should he father a son by a goddess of the old earth-race, as was his wish, would himself fall by the hand of that son. Prometheus, in his desperate need, decided to make use of this knowledge in bringing Zeus to terms.

Under this threat, Zeus forsook the daughter of ancient lineage and engendered a new, semi-divine race of heroes through the woman Io, a purified one, horned, met in the guise of a cow or new moon. Io was the sacramental animal segregated from all creatures of earth to bear the seed of Prometheus' deliverance. She was the ancestress of Heracles, his reconciler, and a long line of heroes. Through these heroes men received a portion of the gods' being, and when this being is the measure, the soul of man may be filled by very little, yet the universe itself cannot contain it. Master-men they become at last.

Prometheus, in forcing Zeus to send an intercessor in his behalf, brought about the necessity for the religious institution of tragic drama, in which a god is made to appear among men as refreshment from Olympus and as a gift of freedom from the awful burdens of Prometheus.

Central to Greek tragic drama was the god-man Dionysus, whom, as with each of the sacramental race, Earth was loath to bear, fearing his mastery. So, he was snatched up and was born a second time in Zeus, whereupon he descended to earth and mingled first with the uncorrupted beasts, who immediately recognized him. Chief among his followers was the goat-man Silenus, who taught that men in their natural state were abandoned creatures, made in mockery of the true, sacramental man. He sang out his own longing for fulfillment through Dionysus. Without illusion or self-deceit he showed himself as a living mockery of the god he desired. He instructed men in the ways of a world which was, after all, but mock scene and drama to the audience of gods, among whom the real drama had been determined from eternity. Yet, he taught, even by this mockery one night engage their attention, their favor, and even their participation.

Silenus and his followers therefore mocked, with their drunken fertility orgies, the life-giving god Dionysus. They mocked the painfulness of their own abundance, mimicked the grotesqueness of their creaturliness, and the god, drawn by the simulation of this powers, first appeared to these animal men, recognizing them as suitable instruments for his words, and he gave in exchange his intoxication.

The god, being most like to the beast in respect to his innocence and fulness, showed himself first to the goat-man. Silenus, god-drunk, informed, made fertile by the god's word, became filled with his harmony like a pipe with wind,, and began singing the lyrics of longing and pure joy which the chorus intones as it portends, heralds, and revels in the coming of the god.

The choral lyric was a magical incantation used by Silenus and his troop to command the presence of Dionysus the twice born, induce him to share his vine of life, and become reborn through him. Their song was thus a deliberate imitation of the god's creative act, and their longing, their drunkenness, and the travail of their lyric were a ferment in which he grew. Then these animal-men, Dionysus' first priests, made mock of their own native fertility and offered it as a goat-sacrifice upon his altar so that they might exchange it for his livingness. The chorus thus mesmerized themselves by him, and the god, in turn, liking the flavor of their offering, approving the wholeness and soundness of the animal, enjoying its taste, accepted and partook of their sacrifice and thereby bound himself to be present in it, to be partaken of by his celebrants. In their mimicry, in the ecstasy and triumph of their lyric, he read, his own parable.

The chorus, who remained throughout the Greek drama essentially priests and priestesses of Dionysus, at whose altar they ministered, officiated at this public festival and were assigned the task of producing on the stage a sacrificial spectacle worthy of the god. The choral song must enchant him, persuade him, conjure him from his human concealment and force him to speak. The song was a travail, the travail of his birth. The chorus became spellbound by him. Like mediums, they then summoned forth on the stage the vision of the god-man, bade him reveal his doings and act out his drama.

The dramatic offering which would find favor with the god must be a high mimicry, as Silenus showed, of man in his natural state. His mock joy at the success of his own worldly contrivances, as if he had obtained some real good, and then his being tripped up in them by Silenus, provoked in the spectators laughter, which is mock joy, and summoned forth the god as revel-leader, wearing the comic mask, to share with the spectators his scoffing, cruel high comedy that spared not men's hopeful schemes and saved them from developing a bad taste for their own "good works." The god and his followers thus communed by a mutual mockery. When the chorus called forth upon its stage high and mighty passions and plans ending in ruin, the spectators wore faces of mourning and the god appeared on the scene in tragic mask, attracted by the parody of his own sorrow. Again the victim, vainly lamenting his grief, and the god were united by mutual mockery and the witnesses partook of the god. The audience, giving laughter and tears—a common mock joy and sorrow—received in exchange a portion of that godly being, of whose joy and suffering in his longing to bestow fulness of life their laughter and tears were but shadows. Dionysus thus purified their taste. He saved them from sympathy with suffering and from delight in mere depravity.

Dionysus was the twice-born, once of woman, to be persecuted and destroyed by men, and again born of his father, to become a sacramental word. He found more purity among the satyrs then in men and used them to introduce his rites. These satyrs found quick acceptance, for when the natural vitality of men is on the wane they show a closer affinity for the animal and a tendency toward aggressive bestiality in their critical longing for health, instinctively coupling health of soul with the condition of animal innocence.

The worship of Dionysus through tragedy was capable of uniting that highly diverse, talented, skeptical, anarchistic, willful Athenian public throughout the period of its unique eminence, and upon the decline of this art Athens, as if suddenly deprived of its healing potion; fell from glory-Dionysus had been the common meal that sustained society.

Yet, all the elements of the crisis had been present when the worship of Dionysus had been introduced—fanatical personal rivalry, free-thinking, political treachery, foreign influences, and the shift from land aristocracy to commercial democracy. It was to a declining society, one becoming religiously remiss, that Dionysus appeared, not as an innovator but as a restorer of his father's worship. His mission was to revivify in men the vision of the higher man by being a sacramental present as the offering of the ritual drama.

A god, yet a man, ambiguous, ironic, self-mocking, Dionysus dies, as a man, in order to scoff, as a god, at all men that consider profitable, useful, virtuous, and correct. He is lawbreaker and misleader. He causes men to stray from their beaten paths, to become blind among familiar scenes, to be proved ignorant in their knowledge, and to feel themselves barren in their fertility. He taught that there was sight, and again sight; hearing, and again hearing. Being of two-fold nature he spoke in parable. The god-man is the living parable.

Dionysus is concealed by his manhood, and he shows himself as a man. As man, he suffers from the richness of his godliness. He desires to be seen, to bestow, and to be known in his word.

Desiring vessels for his overflow, he descended upon the human stage to be sacrificed. Only a man-god could feel this necessity for being partaken of. He was the fire of the vine, needing a culture wherein his virtue could seed. A holy precinct, fenced off from the universe, must be his bestowing place.

The Greek theater was designed as such a sanctuary. It was laid out like an altar for him, Dionysus, gentle physician, the feast of plenty, wine to be spilt on the stone. The taste of him restored the innocent animality of men. He made the human appetite sounder, purer, more bestial, more sensible, more childlike, and more reasonable. He was Dionysus the liberator of men from Promethean chains.

Priests prepared his sanctuary as a screen to exhibit the vision of the music-borne god—for the act of a god sounding himself in the depth of matter is harmony in time, and matter being thus played upon is music taking form as a vision—a screen to intercept and render intelligible his word of light. Dionysus' music was thus the seed of his life planted in the people of his precinct, whose fruit was the vision of the god himself spread as their sacramental feast. In this vision Dionysus, entoned by his priests as the "life-giver," would come to revivify in his precinct the divine scene, conjuring the time when men had once walked with their gods, a scene which, though mere imitation, was a true artistic medium for the double-natured god-man to root his vine. His "scene," accordingly, was no scene of man's own contrivance or familiarity. Man's natural, Promethean scene is the landscape of infinite matter, space unbounded and ungodly, a shifting ground without sure place however-sofar penetrated. The god's precinct would be a fixed point, a place of return, a sun around whence the universe could be moved.

Dionysus was the sacrament that purged the spectator-feasters of their enslavement to the Promethean world. He was their purifier. His wine was their new blood. He delivered them from the Titan curse of brotherhood. He reconciled them to the paternal order and placed them in a state of grace to receive the luminous Olympian crown. Dionysus came with a long line of heroes who brought Olympian gifts to weath Prometheus' work for man. They bestowed the higher Self, the human ego's proper desire, rational social order, which, like light, is external to things but discriminates and encompasses all in its unity; and they planted the roots of rational science as its eternal and true theology.

The Athenian audience therefore expected from tragic drama the real gain that they required from all art. Art was for them the bridge to the higher, sacramental man. In this, their art was "rational." This was their faith in reason: that being themselves but shadows, they could, nevertheless, through imitative ritual make themselves into suitable costumes for the gods' masquerade. Who were a man and not a god they judged go be absurd, a creature empty and alone, pursuing fruitless labors. Greek life was not only permeated by religious art, but it was also hazarded on religion's rationality. In light of this dangerous chance is it astonishing; that the Greeks' time and space were harmonic and proportional measures, that they treated matter as nothing except a screen to exhibit pure, formal geometric image, that they deduced political laws from the music that summoned Dionysus, that living in the gods' precincts they did not feel the earnest sentiment of gravity or the lust for material penetration, that they despised machines and laughed "good works" to scorn, and that they were audacious enough to assert that only the rational man was happy and free? Or does, the wonder lie in the fact that a society was rich enough to pledge its existence on the chance of being at one with its gods—on the happiness of that chance?

Dionysus, in revitalizing Greek religion, was the incarnate word of the gods. Actions that did not reveal their design had no place on the tragic stage where heroes and demigods were brought to the sacrifice. Yet without the chorus, that drama could not have been called forth at all. The drama was the chorus' produced vision, the hero their victim. The chorus formed a priestly medium that conjured Dionysus-to officiate at the ritual as high priest. The victim, on the other hand, the drama's hero, must be of good stock if he is to delight the god's taste sufficiently that the god will enter into him and sanctify him. The hero must be a splendid animal, the consecrated of the flock, mankind's finest specimen. He must possess extraordinary personal power and endowments, he should be a hero or king, if the god is to find him in good taste. It is the awful office of the chorus, then, to lure forth this victim and to assist the god in tracking him down, of wreathing him for sacrifice, of catching him in the labyrinth of his own waywardness, of blinding him with his own conceit of knowledge, of tricking him with his own plans, of humbling him with his own arrogance, and of destroying him with his own power, so that at length he may be taught to mock his existence with his own life, making of it a sacrifice, the god being present in him.

In Aeschylus' tragedy it was the giant figure of man himself, Titan man, in the figure of Prometheus, which the chorus offered up to the god. Calling on Prometheus to divulge to them his deed, the chorus of Oceanids, alternately pitying and feeling terror at his crime, repelled, attracted and mesmerized by him in turn, induced him to speak.

Though all the creatures of earth acknowledged a natural sympathy for Prometheus, they could neither soften his asperity nor pierce the loneliness of this pride. He called out for witnesses to his pain and unjust suffering but rejected with contempt all offers of help or mediation. He took comfort only with lonely, half-mad Io, whose sufferings bore on his. Pregnant with the seed of Zeus' son, Heracles the reconciler, she has been turned away from her father's house and made to wander through unknown wildernesses, a stranger to the earth and pursued by Argus, earth's evil eye. Both are on fire with divine agony for the sake of men. He suffers with immovable chains from the wrath of heaven, she with unresting movement from the wrath of earth. Both are exiles.

Exulting in solitude and chains, glorying in his crime, Prometheus reasserted his absolute rebellion. He chose to serve the rock in a landscape monstrous in its contradictory shiftings from ice to thaw, from mountain peak to abyss, rather than to compromise his pride. He longed for the god's life, yet he would not forego exile if meant the negation of his act. He willed to be master of an eon, even an eon of agony. By his own will was he bound. The more rigid and inescapable Prometheus felt his bonds, the more forcibly he affirmed the inviolability of his pure freedom of will, the quintessence of egotism. And so he remained crucified to a sterile rock. For, had he not made Zeus' fire a sterile force? He lay exposed to hostile winds blowing hot, cold, and contrary. He was lapped by the sea, fire's death. Yet in this desolation Prometheus obtained his desire. Wishing to master the universe he had, by the Fates' just irony, become master of the void. He gloried not in his lot, but in his lack of it. His pride was in his rock. His rock formed an immovable wedge between heaven and earth, and while he lay midway in irons he blocked communion between gods and men.

It was when Zeus sent Hermes, Prometheus' successor, that Prometheus felt the bitterest sting. He saw a new god enjoying the honors of which he was deprived. Prometheus, chained in his desert wildness, caught a glimpse of the fruits for which he hungered and was seized by spite. Never had his own sufferings brought him to such a dangerous point. He had indulged in self-pity and had yearned for sympathy. He was to know utter weariness of spirit. In his punishment he had acknowledged no dishonor, but shame at his felt envy of the god tormented his pride, and as storms churned sky and earth into a chaos moving in on him, he flung a final contemptuous taunt to the master-god. Sinking into the dark emptiness of space and deeper ruin, he still raised his unrepenting voice into oblivion.

Locked now in his ego's windowless prison, Prometheus began forging his own Nemesis. He was weighted by matter's degradation, sucked downward by its gravity, deafened by its ceaseless whirl in void, his thoughts become voiceless echoes. Thus abandoned, he felt his own absurdity. Here was burnt in the minds of all Prometheus' creatures the seductive, memoried image of the rock cutting the infinite, dark vista of space which is Prometheus' domain, outside, beyond, and cut adrift from each godly precinct. Here it was he dreamed out his nightmare of penetrating this wall of space, of mastering this shadow-realm by escaping it. His will-to-power had coiled back on itself and had become, once again, the slave's prayer that he be freed from his toils. This absolute will to freedom was Prometheus' legacy and has become his Nemesis, forging again for him heavy chains. For, Promethean man cannot free himself. H" cannot die to his world. He needs must wait for the coming of the man who can die—the god who is also man.

In Greek drama a unity of action is obtained by virtue of the drama's being in reality a high-communication produced through the art of the chorus-priesthood. It is a vision, a grace to crown their music and ritual incantation, consisting in an already perfected action of a drama divinely written. The result was a surface characterization of apparent simplicity. The Greek hero had no hidden inwardness. Although Greek drama was performed in the open air it could not be produced in any random place. Being a down-going of the god to his altar, its action was confined to his sanctuary.

After the fall of Greek and Roman civilization, the sacramental aspect of tragedy was long cloistered in churches as the Christ symbol, a contradictory fusion of Dionysus with Prometheus—a man-god who could die for the sake of the brotherhood of man. Again men were deprived of that high object of ancient sacrament, the higher Self, which is in essence social and is the basis for rational society and science. The spiritual tension engendered by this dogma of fusion at length broke its confines and emerged from the churches as a secular universal religion of brotherhood, which, far from freeing itself from its inherent paradox, began involving all mankind in its disastrous consequences.

Western drama since classic times, developing separately from the church, attempted the same fusion from the profane side, attempting to make the Promethean man a universal savior. Whereas the character of the Greek tragic hero had a shining transparency and could be summed up by a series of outward gestures and by his changeless formal mask, the later hero, on the contrary, is complex of countenance and opaque of character. The scene of his drama is interior, a cloistered ego set, however, in a landscape unconfined. Hamlet, an internalized Orestes, is no longer capable of a simple deed, but faced with the vista of an infinite field for action is inwardly paralyzed by the paradox of action itself, of action that will be necessarily fateful and at the same time free. His drama is a process taking place within him. Its attention centers about his motives. He is thus of interest only "in himself" and not through any real gain to the audience.

Contrary to the method of Greek tragedy, modern drama stresses both the personal idiosyncrasies of the hero and his basic identity with the rest of humanity. Interest in him is gained by the faculty of sympathy—it is only by chance that he is not someone else, or, in other words, responsibility for his action is assigned to such a wide variety of causes, hereditary, environmental, and fortuitous, that any other person might be charged, in equal justice, with his deed. Having been made common, he is necessarily lowered in stature. He has no longer the capacity for committing the terrible crime for the gain and hurt of men of which the Western culture-god was guilty. He is but peccant or, at worst, merely acts in bad faith and therefore cannot inspire real terror or wonder, for his motives are basically "understandable." Since the time Faust transformed his evil, all of which consisted in seductions from fidelity, into good by good will and good works, the hero's evil deed elicits sympathy rather than dread and awe. Since a share of these responsibilities is taken from him by the communal personality, his deed is not effectively his to give. He has no singular fate, no real doom. Nature is good to him and her instruction consoling. He belongs to the audience, not to the chorus. His communicants are the mass, not a select and inspired band.

Since the hero of modern drama is conceived as the victim of common chance and destiny and his greatest crime ill-will, the interest of the audience is directed toward the progress of his inward struggle with conflicting motives of egotism and communal fidelity, the motives which guide his course in the infinite field given for his action. He is no longer permitted to come to grip with the profound paradox resulting from Prometheus' crime. He merely engages a problem orthodox communal humanity, with time and understanding, will ostensibly solve through its Inquisitorial prerogatives. It will simply wash the paradox from its body with confessed streams of words. Therefore the problem presented in a modern drama cries each time for re-solution because it cannot, like the Prometheus tragedy, undertake the real fact of crime and human crisis.

For, of what gain is it to confess the crime—if the crime is no gain?

Our human scene is defaced by the babbling confessings of bad actors and our language traduced.

Our human scene is now overrun by the Titan brotherhood of Prometheus' cycle, and his Nemesis, the Modern Spirit of our times, has taken over the rubble of Dionysus' altar for the purpose of obverting the one crime he could not digest—the return of Greek drama's sacramental hero to unseat him. Sterily he presides over the modern scene, leading his votaries inexorably towards the path where Prometheus found them "rushing headlong into death." Under his guidance men, as if entranced with their own extinction, race feverishly toward their doom, perverting the arts and sciences bestowed by Greek religion, to the and that Prometheus must lie so heavily chained that only universal destruction will put him out of his agony. Thus the paradoxical dogma which holds that the brotherhood of man in its perfectible spatial and temporal totality is the true sacramental body has resulted in intolerable crisis as the brothers, in love's name, pursue the dark and bloodthirsty division of their inheritance, each finding his portion to be only a progress, a bridge leading into the endless, enticing landscape of their common ground.

This drama directed by the promethean Nemesis is acted out by the modern mass-man with all the outward optimism incumbent upon his efficiency. As he becomes more isolated and atomized in the social mass his beliefs become articulated in terms of social forces. Yet as he obtains unlimited means of communication he loses social communion. As his conception of space and time is extended his world vision contracts into a well-conditioned world of ways and means, and into the privacy of his horns, with its clutter of orderliness, he carries the spiritual chaos of his aloneness. Each heir to Prometheus is chained to a rock of solitude. Self-immolated, without spiritual paternity, he must either surpass himself or become submerged in an animal-like existence.

The predicament of this modern mass-man characterizes him at every level of the social scale: mania for enlightenment, specialized tasks, isolation, and anxiety at being alone. Bereft of purpose, he puts faith in the common future, yet he himself carries no futurity. Sympathetic, irritable, curious, and desiring to be informed about his neighbor, he makes use of a language increasingly denotative and abstract, suitable as an instrument of technical guidance for getting through the day and for filtering down orders and commands relating to methods of doing things in efficient ways. His science is formulated in terms of the predictable behavior of masses and the incidence of chance eccentricity; to be informed on his destiny he must speak statistics. In lonely panic he demands continuing crises to fill void days and make them pass and perverts his pursuit of happiness into pursuit of happenings, watching for fateful signs in the news. Instead of seeking to create of himself a higher, rational instrumentality, he attempts to identify himself with some successful program or plan. Claiming rights as nature's heir he purposes to render society altogether "natural," and so his good works multiply on the basis of the common body of knowledge of how to do "things," as he militantly lays the foundations for a brute society whose language will be instinctively informational, and to whom the problem of objective truth will offer only archaeological interest. Thus, in his lust for enlightenment in ways and means to comprehend and organize the world, the mass-man abdicates the throne of reason and condemns himself to a scene of spiritual twilight.

This well-ordered yet singularly lost and aimless mass forms the audience of our modern theatre. It demands, impatiently, its banquet of the eye, its feast of spectacles. In its fear of isolation and in its need for felt companionable warmth it flocks together in disciplined mildness. Nevertheless it ravens after its sights like a pack that has found a common prey. Its curiosity, readily stimulated, easily diverted, being mob-appetite, is astonishingly versatile. The mass would know everything, particularly about the predicament of its fellows. It wills to know, without owning individual responsibility for its knowledge. This quality of disinterest is, too, identical on every level of mass society on its "knowing." The aggressive curiosity of the man on the street and that of the man of science are equally pure of personal expectation. Both men share the deeply rooted conviction that they must collect diverse, descriptive information as an act of good will toward the common body comprising the consensus of brothers, which alone will be able to comprehend its vast factual manifold. Both thus avow faith in the "scientific method" which has prepared their way of life so smoothly and with such irrevocable enlightenment.

This common faith sets the mood and atmosphere and summons forth the drama of our theatre. The audience is compassionate and inquisitional. It appoints itself an eager and impartial confessional for the protagonists of the scene, upon which it casts its spotlight with merciless clarity. The mass wills only to "know," and neither wishes nor hopes for any personal advantage from the action. Its pleasure is rather just to ruminate over it and, with the warm glow of its sympathy, to administer a tender lash to those victims of disorientation who appear on the scene, guiding them thus back on the right path. The audience remains, for all its feeling of shared guilt, radically innocent, irresponsible, and safe from the drama, capable of engorging all possible evil though its abysmal understanding. All its pleasure is in just in "knowing," and its moral elevation is attained through a tacit belief that it can purify the scene by receiving the confessions of the actors.

Yet, what indeed does this knowing, this common eye, require of the actors on its stage? To whom is their language addressed, what spirit invoked? What quality of mind enlightens the scene? How could that higher man withstand its glare?

The eye, image of reason and maker of reason's images, is kept chaste by reason, which is the spiritual palate for god-essence. The evil eye of the Modern Spirit, however, has turned reason aside from its rightful object and has evoked an image unequaled in monstrosity by any of old fable. On the analogy of reason, he has postulated a universal being, as god, state, idea, as the fictitious father of the brotherhood of man and as the son-spouse of Maya. Whereas by Prometheus' sacrifice the father-god was cheated of his sons, the Modern Spirit offers men a spurious father in the concept of a being who incarnates their brotherhood and whose will is to possess, comprehend, and create and become manifest through matter. This is pure egotism conceived as deity. It is an analogous rational goal used to convince men of their "rationality" and it is a surrogate god used to obliterate in men all memory of the sacred Classicism of their past. It is now ripening to fulness under the eye and genius of our Modern Spirit, that ghoul of retribution lurking in Prometheus' crime. This Nemesis is but an emasculated shadow of the mighty criminal, yet his feeble strength is equal to his task of seeing to its conclusion the Promethean cycle, since he encounters scarcely any resistance the world over.

Whereas Greek science disdained as its proper pursuit the comprehension of matter, but instead deduced from essential definitions a base upon which the material world; could rest as rational image, the theology adhering to the universal being has been directed toward the search for a general force acting on matter and a principle of energy comprehending all mass, such energy-force being conceived as manifesting the will of a universal existence. It is this theology, in which is comprised the methods, of physical science, that gives its philosophical foundation of egotism to modern society.

The god of reason, Self, that most ancient of Aryan gods, the master, was external to man, like light, and being; social, could be obtained only through the language of society. Every Greek god bespoke this Self, and therefore dialogue like drama meant to the Greeks a joyous banquet and Holy Communion. It was a shared feast, through which they attained individual mastery and social order. Through dialogue they tasted a god.

The Modern Spirit has peeled off this external unifying grace of science and society and has replaced it by a fictive internal principle of unity, whereby like units of force cohering through a field men must conglomerate, their mere existence conceived as a social force, into a spatio-temporal relation as separate points of ego-energy. They belong not to ordered society, but they are amalgamated into an analogous society of mass, which is but a collection of identical ego-forces, whose co-existence is conceived as compelling their unity. In this collective ego-centered society the basic relationship between man and man is necessarily one of radical violence, both repulsive and attractive. Such a Promethean society is a conceptual paradox.

For, as a point of force has no real center comprehending both its position and motion but is in this respect dual, so is the ego a false center of personality. It is a mere part of an analogous unified field which is itself a mere collection of parts. It finds no point of rest or return, no memory base, in this "internal unity." The individual ego, when cut off from its true center in Self, needs must fall from its essence. In its unceasing moral and intellectual deviation from its center it loses its ground in rational society. It forms a field for motion. It is therein that man falls infinitely downward toward material existence. Losing his "definition" he decreases steadily in stature and becomes a man of the mass. He wills to forget who he is. Without purpose, he puts his faith in future happiness, yet he is not capable of a future. Ha is fit only to receive rules that will enable him to function in the limits given by his environment. Happiness is laid out for him in many gravelled paths but he no longer owns any fate. He lacks power for good or ill. He is savagely innocent. Authority and responsibility become diffusely scattered through the entire mass organization and therefore exist only fictitiously, in the guise of a universal mass tyranny, which enjoins that the individual, cut off from his true center, is perforce obliged to be free.

Left alone with his freedom, the individual knows the misery of his abandonment. He discovers himself tricked, freighted with matter, and begins to abominate himself as a freak and buffoon of the Modern Spirit. He is the product of ancient betrayal. The paths leading therefrom to universal suicide are various, inevitable, and even well-ordered.

Men thus isolated and ego-directed become increasingly conditioned by their field of motion to expend themselves within natural limits, like plants or animals, to exfoliate, as if produced by some infinite hypothetical syllogism of pure being, into appearances. They are increasingly compelled to become things. These individual units cannot form a society; they can only be fused into a mass.

Thus the human community becomes spiritually empty as its social organization increases in complexity. The mass coheres through atomization. Its language, reduced to a technical apparatus, moves and conditions it in terms of force and matter. Through its collective base of radically separate but morally identical particles connected by inherent force, the mass becomes homogeneous in appearance and warm with mutual recognition of lonely predicaments in its common awareness of being trapped. It is quick to sympathize and to mimic. It fuses through feeling. Yet it is compassionately indifferent to itself. Lacking common spiritual bread its members remain fundamentally alien to each other, though all voice the belief that social union can be achieved eventually through technological effort, wherein each may fulfill himself as a unique dimension. As discrete particles they are homeless and exiled from rational order, and though the mass morality ordains that a place be made for each, its house, lacking the pillars of reason to support authority, is insufficient to shelter a society. It but provides an open field. It has shrunk to a hive of indefinitely extensible cells, the ultimate containment of free egos regarded as moral ends. Its full authority is simply "in itself," a connective function shared and perpetuated by all its members by virtue of their existence as forces. Governed thus internally, this surrogate society is an infinitely open system of induction of members into its collection, but it is formally closed.

With the ground for social order eroded the basis for language slips away. Dialogue with the spirit of pure egotism is an impossibility. One can but tender it one's own bit of monologue. So essentially cut off from discourse, the mass-man is condemned to perpetual aloneness. Lacking spiritual center, he experiences an animal terror at the space he must traverse in his comprehension of the material universe and a human terror of the endless time that measures his solitudinous path. The terrible fact of his existence is that he is lone, free, and fateless, an ultimate thing-in-itself moving into void and speaking into abysmal silence. As an individual he cannot survive. He is without language.

He thus becomes a votary of the Modern Spirit of language which, wearing the mask of Self, proffers him a spurious sacrament of speech, a logic derived from analogues of ideas—the concept of classes of events. The members of these classes obtain meaning not from a realm of essence, but they are conceived as freely bound events being united into a term through their own inner force. Since the only definition for such a class is an entailing force of the class "in itself," a field relation between members, its concept is basically dual. There is no center for a class of events to-rest on. Its concept renders even a tautology contradictory. Thus the paradox rooted in an ego-centered society reappears in modern logic.

This logic thus has no principle of self-consistency. Its implicit aim is to yield formulas of necessary entailment of itself, to achieve its own self-binding through future events. It becomes a monologue that ever only tends to approach self-proof, for it lacks essential terms. It forms the basis for a wholly natural language that can suck the mass-man into dogmatic obedience to its tenet that truth always waits to be produced by his corporate brotherhood. Thus the speech of the mass-man becomes a collection of individual monologues conceived as contributing to the infinite monologue of pure being, the comprehensive summation of all speech parts at some distant time. The Modern Spirit is engaged in conditioning men to spiritual silence so that a uniform technique of inquiry may be perfected for the increase and consumption of information in a purely technological universe of discourse, the ultimate monologue of spirit voided into matter.

Faith in the perfectibility of this inquisitorial monologue forms in the mass its ground for unanimity and optimism in a commonly held future. The mass, in merely being a consensus of witnesses of events, arrogates to itself, in the name of this being's perfect self-proof and in abrogation of reason, the ultimate tribunal of verification. Thus language, like society, grounded in the production of existent things, becomes fragmented. The mass-man serves merely as machinery for channeling information into a common sink. Since the "thingness" of a thing is best communicated by shared sensations of witnesses, language becomes intensified as sense-signs attaching to events. Its communicants become sensitives instead of thinkers. They are turned, by their nature-logic, toward matter as sympathetic witnesses of its manifold appearance. They are used s a choral medium through which is conducted the aberrated duet of universal being with matter, the resonance f its monologue. Their thought, turned aside from reason, made into a self-binding machinery for going through matter, spiritualizing it into dimension. Since matter can be penetrated only by taking one part of it after the other, in units of time, the fashioning of the yardstick time as a universal measure parallels the sensitizing of thought as j tool of knowledge. Inasmuch as infinite time is the vehicle if the universal monologue, the time problem lies at the heart of modern logic as offering its sole condition of proof. Rootless time, conditioning the future in producing it, yet has no direction in the past, and the forward-looking urge of our uprooted mass-man induces a social amnesia consistent with the aims of an egotistic society that holds al' spiritual pain to be evil heritage from the past. Past history is thence reconceived as having been but an excrescence, a sport, a mere direction, tentative and obscure, largely misdirection, of time's onward stride, and the time-serving language of the mass man, draining his memory of objective truth, shakes him free from intellectual agony by conditioning him as a sensitive conductor of the product-future. Animal organization is thus being accomplished without reference to truth, and a technical, denotative language is being perfected in efficiency even while the principles of its formation elude definition.

His existential language having rendered him a spiritual mute and his many-voiced enlightenment having blinded him to the meaning of his own existence, the mass-man experiences, nevertheless, an increasingly dire hunger for his bread. He wants his sacramental meal spread before him. He wants a vision produced on his stage. He wants a taste of universal being. He wants something to wake him up from his bad dream of falling uncontrollably into the future as he whimpers shrilly: "what makes man, what makes love, necessary?"

In hope of this clarifying grace he tenders on the sacrificial altar none other than himself, in the name of all. Accordingly, he proffers himself for due purification. Since the universal being incarnate in the brotherhood is conceived as alone infallible and absolutely chastening because of its putative self-perfection in time, each brother acknowledges the duty

97

of standing in its spotlight. Yet, since each also regards the other not only as a rival claimant hostile, separated by an iron curtain of root-ego, but also as a moral end-in-himself, a carrier of universal ego-force by which all men will be bound in the common sacramental body, each brother is obliged, in turn, to become the sacrifice. No single one is capable of bearing the responsibility for all. Only universal force can establish the brotherhood. The responsibility lies in their totality. Therefore each brother has also the duty of submitting the other to the purifying inquisition of faith to obtain the common bread of their vision.

Even while his memory is being purged of the Classic, sacramental base of society, with its language, science, and art that atoned for Prometheus' crime, each is being prepared to pay a terrible retribution for his forgetfulness, as the myth of Prometheus, buried in oblivion, rears itself hugely and proceeds to its fulfillment in the full glare of our enlightenment. Men rush, with prurient haste, to embrace its vision. The ancient myth of the fateless ones, the patricides, is being told to the end through the actors themselves, all unknowingly in their knowledge and however unwillingly in their willingness. The amnesia provoked by the mass-man's culture makes for his general optimism in the face of the myth's fruition, yet the unspeakable past is abysmally known by each prisoner as he divines, discomfortingly, that the spoils of a crime somewhere underlie his pleasant paths and his good things of life. So, in order to bring to pass the vision of this, his last act, the Modern Spirit who directs our scene must see to it that the common language is cleansed from any vestiges of essence and that men will be purified of all traces of sacramental mythos from which they, with occasional insight, might suffer and by which their faith in him might be seduced, in order that they may be kept ignorantly pure in their role of producing, with their common body, the vision of Prometheus eternally bound.

For this purpose of moral and mental purgation the autobiographical confession has been institutionalized on our linguistic scene. Each individual in his social abandonment in the mass yet needs suffer mounting anxiety at being separated from it. He undertakes his confession as an act of faith and fusion. The mass, constituted as the audience, demands his complete submission. It views him with personal detachment yet with keen interest. With its Argus eye it pursues him like a pathologist. It requires that he use the idiom of naturalistic mimicry so that the symptoms of his alienation may be feelingly understood and his words, by attaching to the proliferating novelty of his sensations, may produce a gently laxative effect, leaving him without a tale of his own to tell, leaving him a clown of himself, leaving him a pure man of the mass.

Through its disinterested passion for its actor, then, the audience enjoys knowledge of his evils without contamination, since, in its status of a confessional, it runs off meanings of words into channels of waste and clarifies the guilty scene. This ever-willing audience is an irresistible invitation to the performer to make a showing of himself as incarnate liberator and word of truth, and thus are our actors encouraged to apply themselves to the mortifying "good works" of language for the indulgence of general bid taste; in claiming that they are regenerated through their own illumination and that they can give true accounts of themselves, they desecrate language, they blaspheme, and they give the audience false communion in the unsavory spectacle of depravity sympathetically presented.

Habits of sympathy promote D precocious sensitivity to pleasure and pain and a vast capacity for vicarious feeling. The bulk of his knowledge about the human state is derived from this capacity of the mass-man for easy simulation. He is an insatiable, omniverous spectator of his scene and he accordingly "knows" joy and suffering by his feeling appreciation of their outward signs. His lore thus reduces the human agony to a condition of physical pain and represents joy as the state of animal bliss. And as he finds only listless, worried joy in his delights, he likewise finds no purification through his pains. His vision of his agony consists in the ennui and bitteruess of his disillusionment. He is alone with his body and uneasy with it. His bad taste nauseates him. His abstention from the desired pleasures of savagery emasculates him. Could he but rid himself of his bad conscience he would prepare the moral way for an animal society. This is the true desire born of his exhaustion. He has found his freedom a monstrous, unthinkable void, and he has learned n language by which he can conjure on his stage aught but the self-confessing spectre of bad taste. He is an empty vessel and can find nothing with which to refresh himself, for his Modern Spirit is impotent and can but keep guard, unlovingly, amused, watching the betrayal inherent in universal brotherhood bloom under his dark sun as the "brothers" come to the final, violent division of their spoils.

Thus man, left to his natural devices becomes a brute that has lost its innocence and therefore its hope of godliness. He is once more the primitive Titan man "rushing headlong into death" for whom Prometheus perpetrated his great crime. Yet Prometheus lies in chains while his Nemesis presides with evil enjoyment over the uneasy reveries imaged on our human stage. Worldly he is and altogether a hedonist and his justice puts *rat-n* out of reach of tragedy. He is beyond offence, for the confession is a sauce that makes any dish good to his palate and every carnival acceptable. This monster is present universally, self-mocking in his knowledge that in his inviolable chastity as has made crime impotent. He watches only that his actors never be seduced into heresy against him.

To the actor in his solitude the human scene becomes a bestiary inducing communion on an animal level, and his pleasure is taken in natural license. The audience, as the incorporate Modern Spirit presiding on its stage, permits and encourages the appearance of bestial freedom, not in the form of Silenus' mockery but as blandishments to poor appetite. The actor is led to develop a tender palate for his animal nature, with the expectation that its being confessed will cleanse-him of any actual *vice*. To possess knowledge of without capacity for bestiality and to have a nice feeling for moral delinquency—to enjoy without indulging appetite is his public prerogative. Though his knowledge is a bar to his innocence, his evoked vision of bliss assumes an animal nature. It is refreshment: from the tension of speech. Animals do commune silently. His vision may resemble an animal dream but he looks on it with "knowledge" thereof. He develops a moist tongue and an evil eye. His Silenus is no longer innocent. In short, there is no joy in his pleasure and he takes his delights with a bad taste. In consequence of his predicament of aloneness and his informed technique of living, his abrogation of reason, and the mass conspiracy against the emergence of a higher, fateful man, he desperately seeks communion with his fellows in a conceived realm of pure, primal lawlessness from which, however, his knowledge eternally bars him. Furthermore, he regards his lonely, meditated visions as evil, yet their confession as good. Our actors thus play a game wherein they remain radically free of evil upon its being artistically staged before an understanding and humanely chastising audience that watches, with malign delight, secure in its own legal innocence.

Yet, if man would be saved he must become pure and bestial once more. Otherwise, he comes to the end of his story.

If he is to regain health he must feast at another table. He must strengthen his appetite and purge his diet of pity-and-fear sauce. He must shun sympathy and human warmth.

Let him take his abasement back to the barren rock, and let him wear out the rock with watching. Every place but his rock has lost its meaning. Let him become an outlaw of the night.

Let him give battle to the Modern Spirit and indict him for his sly, cheating joke on the fateless ones.

Let him never consent to play a part on his scene.

For, the actor at our confessional invokes himself alone, speaks for himself alone, and forces himself to act. His final depraved role is that he becomes only an actor of himself, in obedience to that Divine Malice, the Modern Spirit, who officiates at the self-devouring sacrifice of all the brothers. Feasting alone in tasteless reverie he sings his chorale of brotherhood and waits for the Titanic drama to end, condoning in advance his actors' most quaint crimes in return for the amusing show they put on of their mutual extermination through their severally held universal patents of righteousness.

Thus he squats on Dionysus' ruined altar. Mutilated Sileni lie in the dust at his feet, laughing at the sun, and the hallowed bones of the god's precinct are bared to the elements.

About the Author

Marjorie Burke lives in La Jolla, California. She has published a book on the origin of history, essays, verse and translations of Greek drama and poetry.